Contents

What is Hanukkah?

Hanukkah is a celebration.

It is the Jewish festival of lights.

Celebrations

...kah

Gillis

www.raintreepublishers.co.uk
Visit our website to find out more information about **Raintree** books.

To order:
 Phone 44 (0) 1865 888112
Send a fax to 44 (0) 1865 314091
 Visit the Raintree Bookshop at **www.raintreepublishers.co.uk** to browse our catalogue and order online.

First published in Great Britain by Raintree, Halley Court, Jordan Hill, Oxford OX2 8EJ, part of Harcourt Education.
Raintree is a registered trademark of Harcourt Education Ltd.

© Harcourt Education Ltd 2003
First published in paperback in 2004
The moral right of the proprietor has been asserted.

Editorial: Jennifer Gillis (HL-US) and Diyan Leake
Design: Sue Emerson (HL-US) and Michelle Lisseter
Picture Research: Amor Montes de Oca (HL-US)
Production: Lorraine Hicks

Originated by Dot Gradations
Printed and bound in China by South China Printing Company

ISBN 1 844 21522 9 (hardback)
07 06 05 04 03
10 9 8 7 6 5 4 3 2 1

ISBN 1 844 21527 X (paperback)
08 07 06 05 04
10 9 8 7 6 5 4 3 2 1

British Library Cataloguing in Publication Data
Gillis, Jennifer
Hanukkah
394.2'67
A full catalogue record for this book is available from the British Library.

Acknowledgements
The publishers would like to thank the following for permission to reproduce photographs: Art Resource pp. 5 (Giraidon), 7 (Image Select), 23 (Temple, Image Select); Corbis pp. 10 (Owen Franken), 11 (Mark Thiessen), 14 (Owen Franken), 21 (Laura Dwight), 23 (latke, Owen Franken); David R. Frazier p. 9; Heinemann Library p. 23 (shamash, Michael Brosilow); Index Stock Imagery pp. 15 (Greg Smith), 22 (Shaffer-Smith), 23 (gelt, Greg Smith; menorah, Shaffer-Smith), 24 (Shaffer-Smith), back cover (gelt, Greg Smith); Lawrence Migdale pp. 4, 8, 16; PhotoEdit, Inc. pp. 12 (Michael Newman), 17 (Michael Newman), 18 (Bill Aron), 20 (Michael Newman), 23 (kippah, Michael Newman); Richard T. Nowitz pp. 19, 23 (dreidel, Hebrew writing), back cover (dreidel); TRIP p. 13 (S. Shapiro)

Cover photograph of lighting a menorah, reproduced with permission of Tudor Photography

Some words are shown in bold, **like this.** You can find them in the glossary on page 23.

Hanukkah is when Jewish people remember a time long ago.

They won a war and took back a building called the **Temple**.

When do people celebrate Hanukkah?

NOVEMBER						
					1	2
3	4	5	6	7	8	9
10	11	12	13	14	15	16
17	18	19	20	21	22	23
24	25	26	27	28	29	30

DECEMBER						
1	2	3	4	5	6	7
8	9	10	11	12	13	14
15	16	17	18	19	20	21
22	23	24	25	26	27	28
29	30	31				

Each year, Hanukkah starts on a different day.

It lasts for eight days and nights in November or December.

The eight days remind Jewish people of the oil lamps in the **Temple**.

Just a little bit of oil lasted for eight days.

What do people do during Hanukkah?

People get together with their family and friends.

They decorate their houses.

There are special food, songs and games.

There may be Hanukkah parties.

What lights are there at Hanukkah?

menorah | shamash

People put candles in a **menorah**.

They light them with a candle called a **shamash**.

Each night, people light one more candle.

Some menorahs are electric!

What do Hanukkah decorations look like?

Hanukkah decorations can be many colours.

People make cut-out candles and **menorahs**.

People make candles and menorahs out of paper or cloth.

What food do people eat at Hanukkah?

People eat **latkes** during Hanukkah.

They are potato pancakes cooked in oil.

People also eat Hanukkah **gelt**.

Hanukkah gelt is chocolate wrapped in gold to look like money.

How do people dress for Hanukkah?

Some people wear their best clothes.

Other people wear jeans and tops.

kippah

Some people wear a **kippah**.

A kippah is a small cap.

What game do people play during Hanukkah?

Children play the **dreidel** game.

They can win sweets or money.

A dreidel is a spinning top with four sides.

Each side has a letter in **Hebrew writing**.

Who gives presents at Hanukkah?

Families and friends give each other presents.

Some families give presents each night of Hanukkah.

Some children make presents to give to their family.

Quiz

What are these Hanukkah things called?

Look for the answers on page 24.

? ? ? ?

Glossary

dreidel
(DRAY-dl) a spinning top with four sides

gelt
chocolate wrapped to look like money

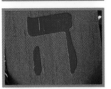
Hebrew writing
the letters used to write Jewish words

kippah
a small cap

latke
(LAHT-keh) potato pancake

menorah
(min-OHR-uh) a special candlestick for the eight days of Hanukkah

shamash
(SHA-mash) the candle in the middle of a menorah

Temple
the building that the Jews won back in a war a long time ago

Index

Answers to quiz on page 22

presents | gelt | dreidel | menorah